The Fair

Written by Becca Law
Illustrated by Carol Herring

RISING ★ STARS

It is a fair.

Get a ticket and off we go!

Get to the top of the big slide!

Sit on the mat and off we go!

Get in the bumper car!

Ram into Mum and ram into Dad!

Pick up a duck to win!

Hit the cans to win!

The man sells big bags of popcorn.

Pick up a bag and off we go!

Talk about the book

Ask your child these questions:

1 What did the children go on first at the fair?
2 How did the children get down from the top of the big slide?
3 Who did the children ram into with their bumper cars?
4 How can the family win a prize at the fair?
5 Which ride from the book would you like to go on?
6 Have you ever been to a fair? Was it fun?